Clare Fennell

The Boy and the Ball

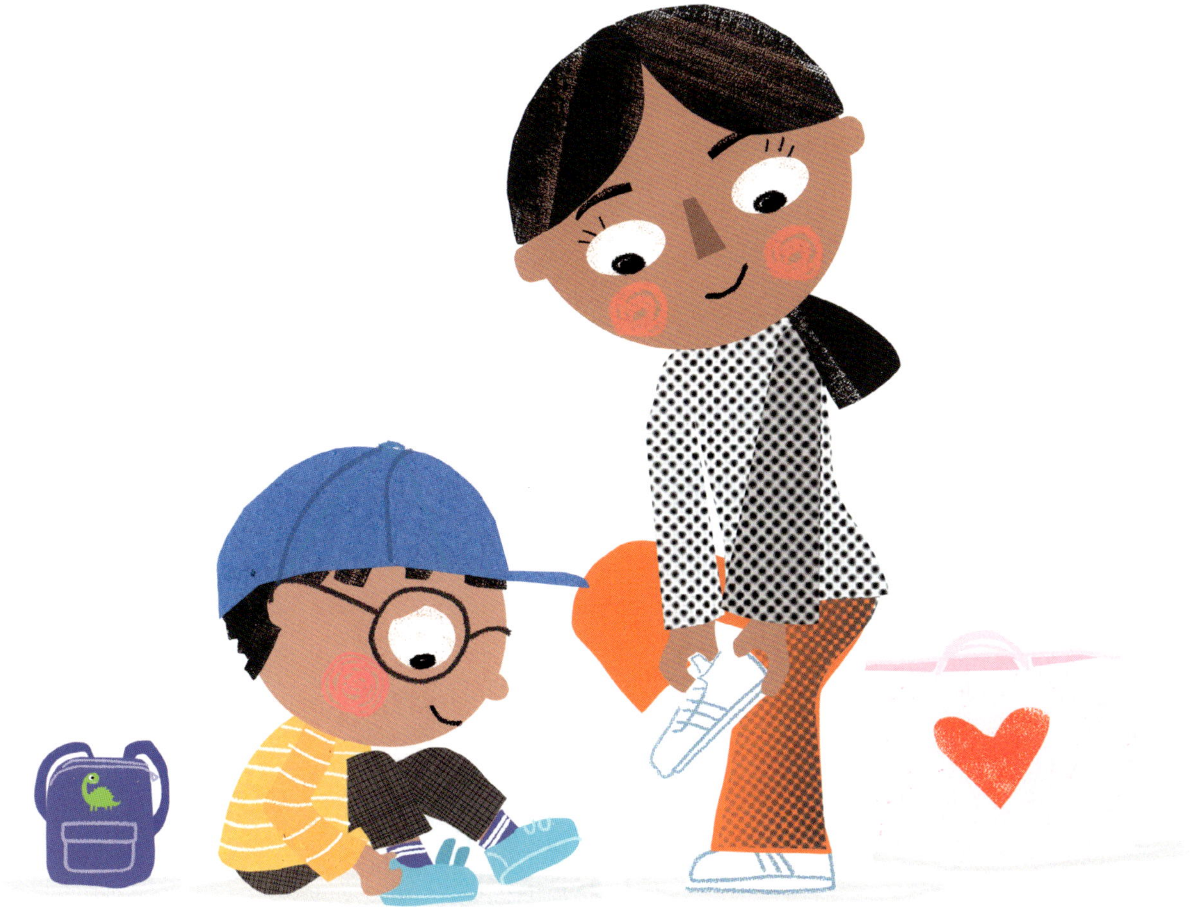

Collins

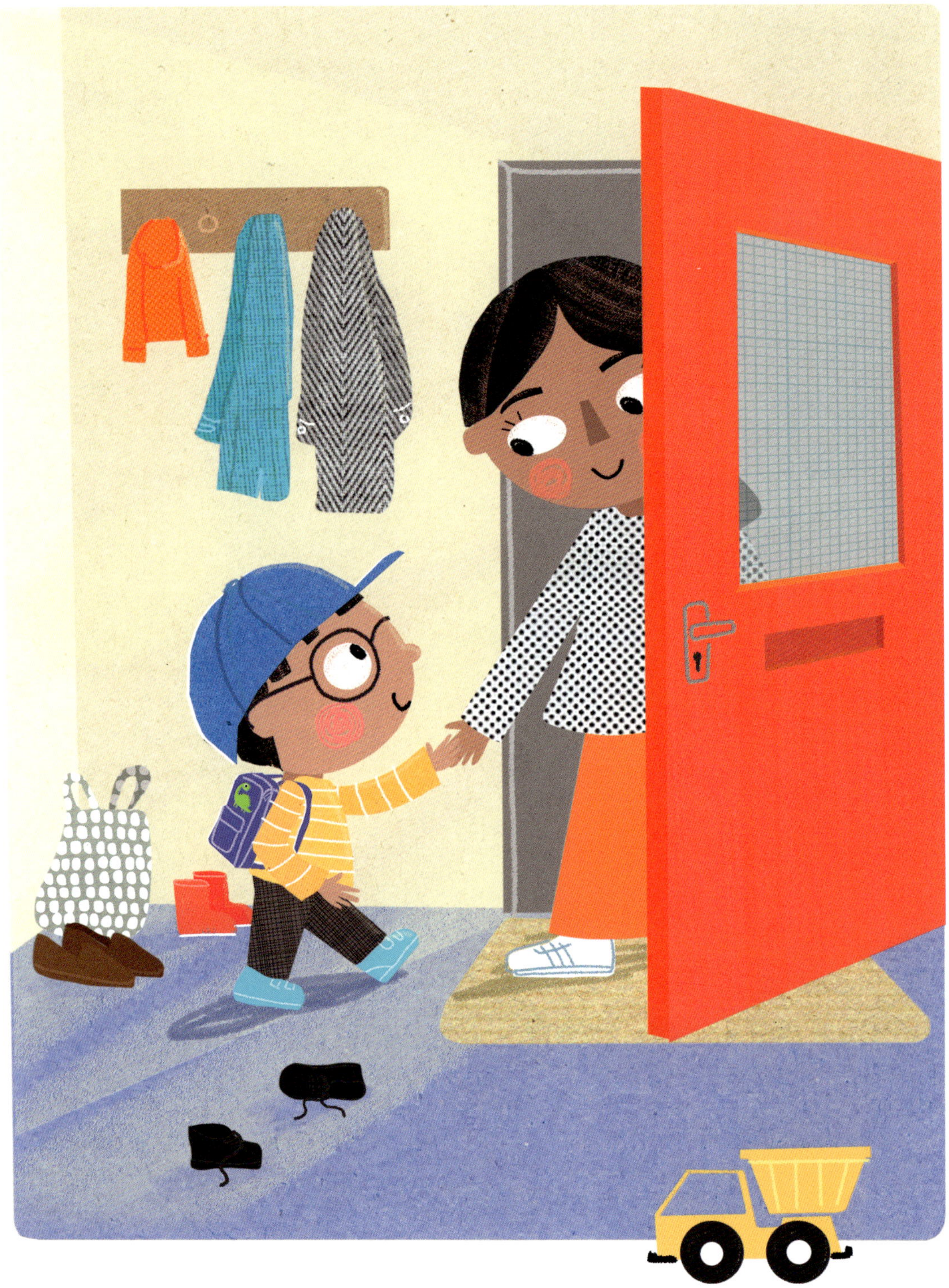

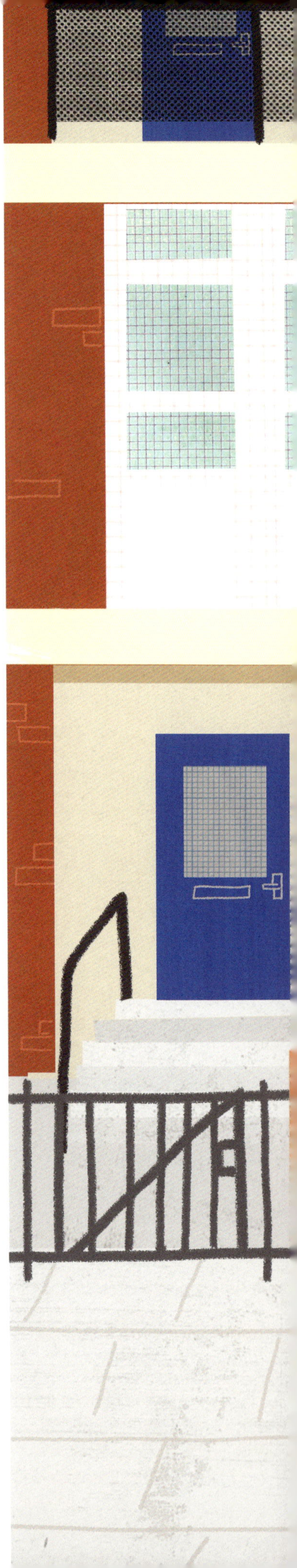

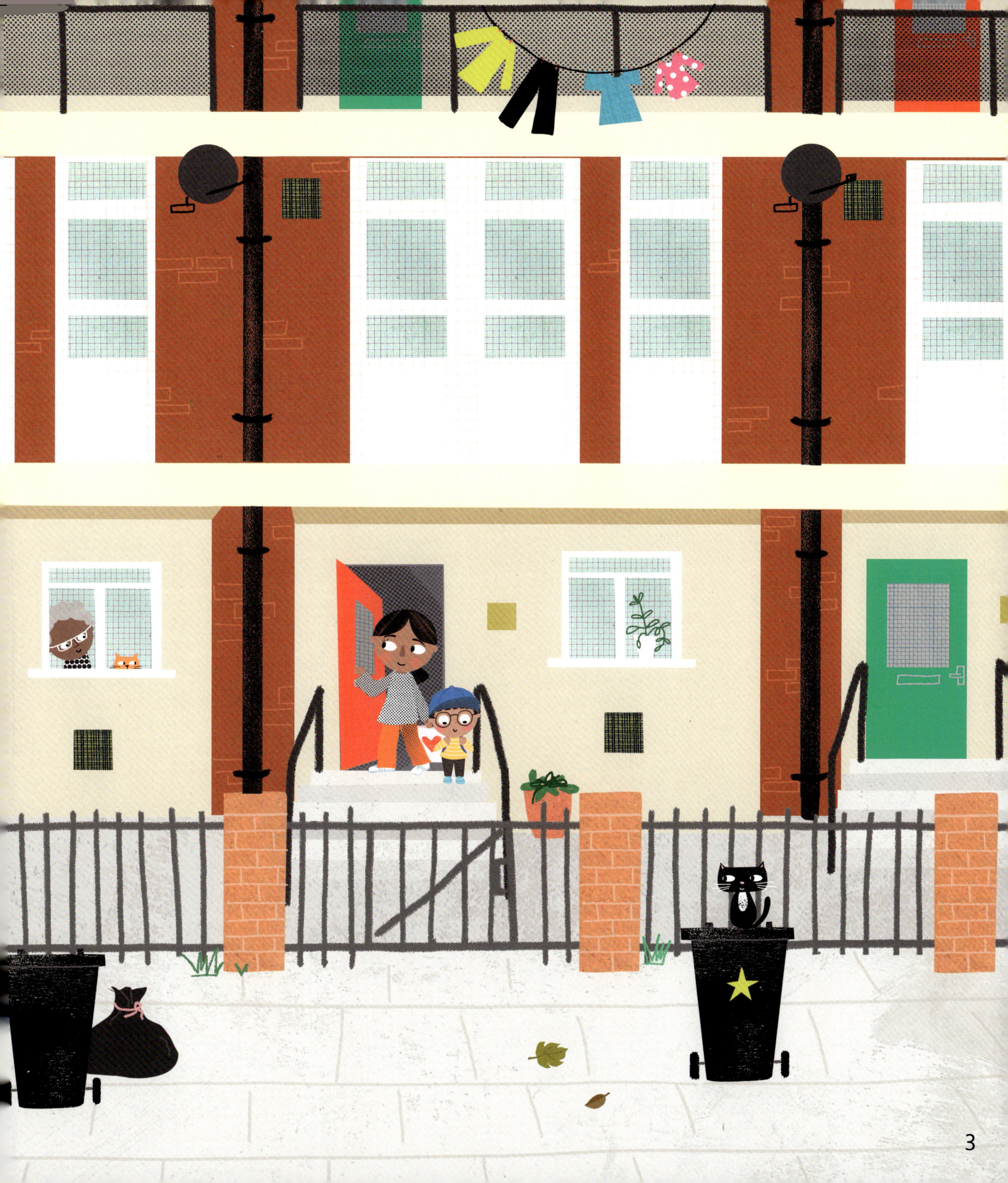

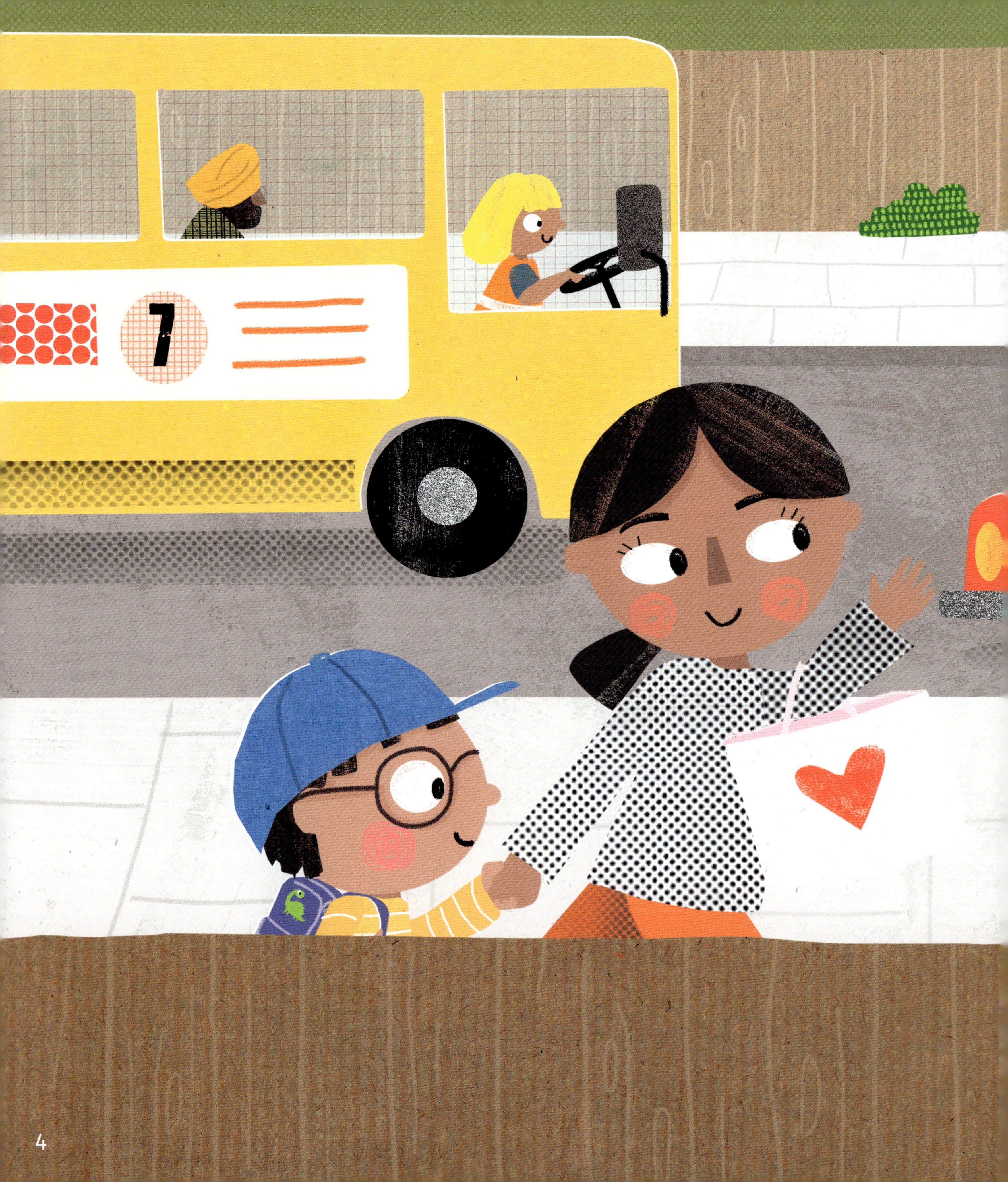
7

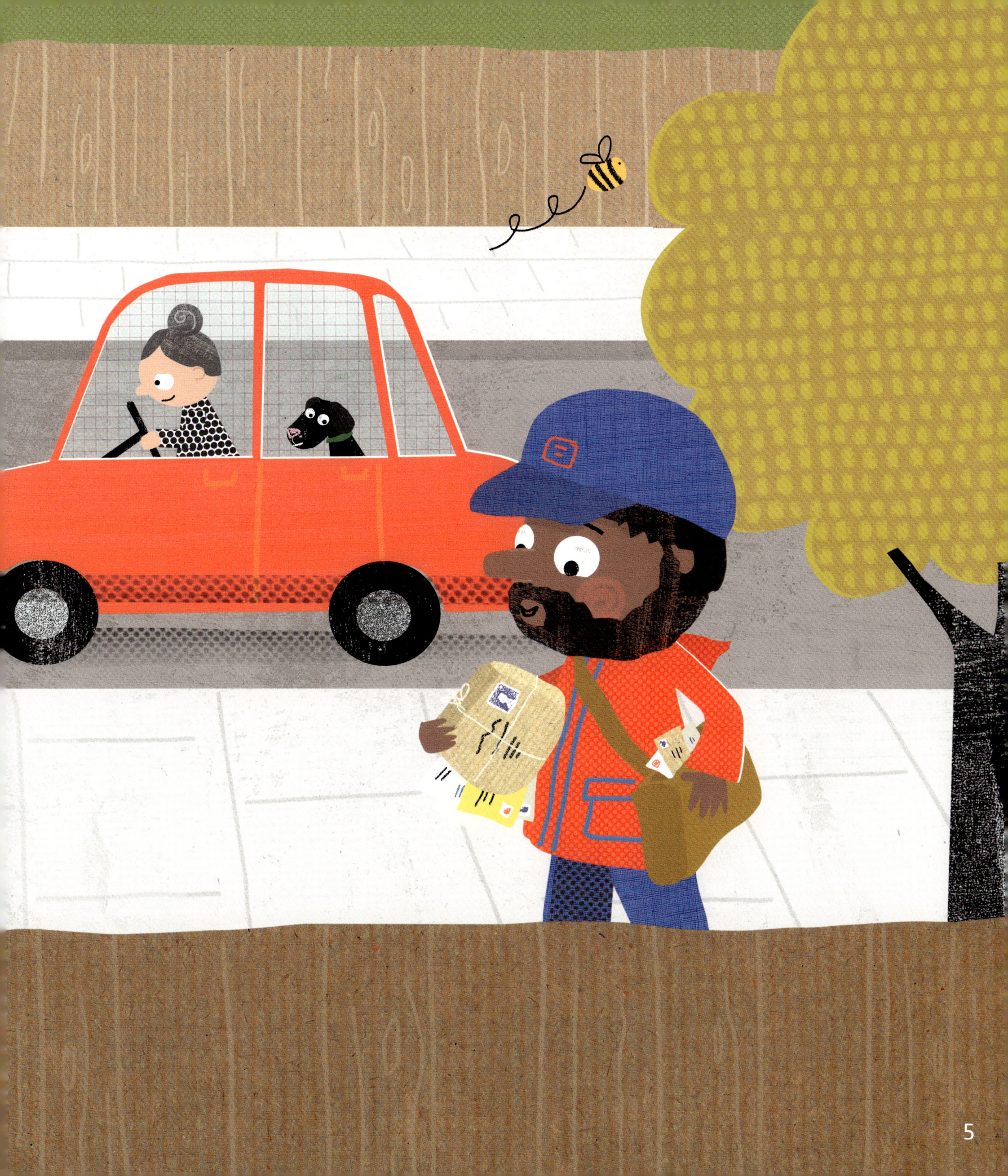

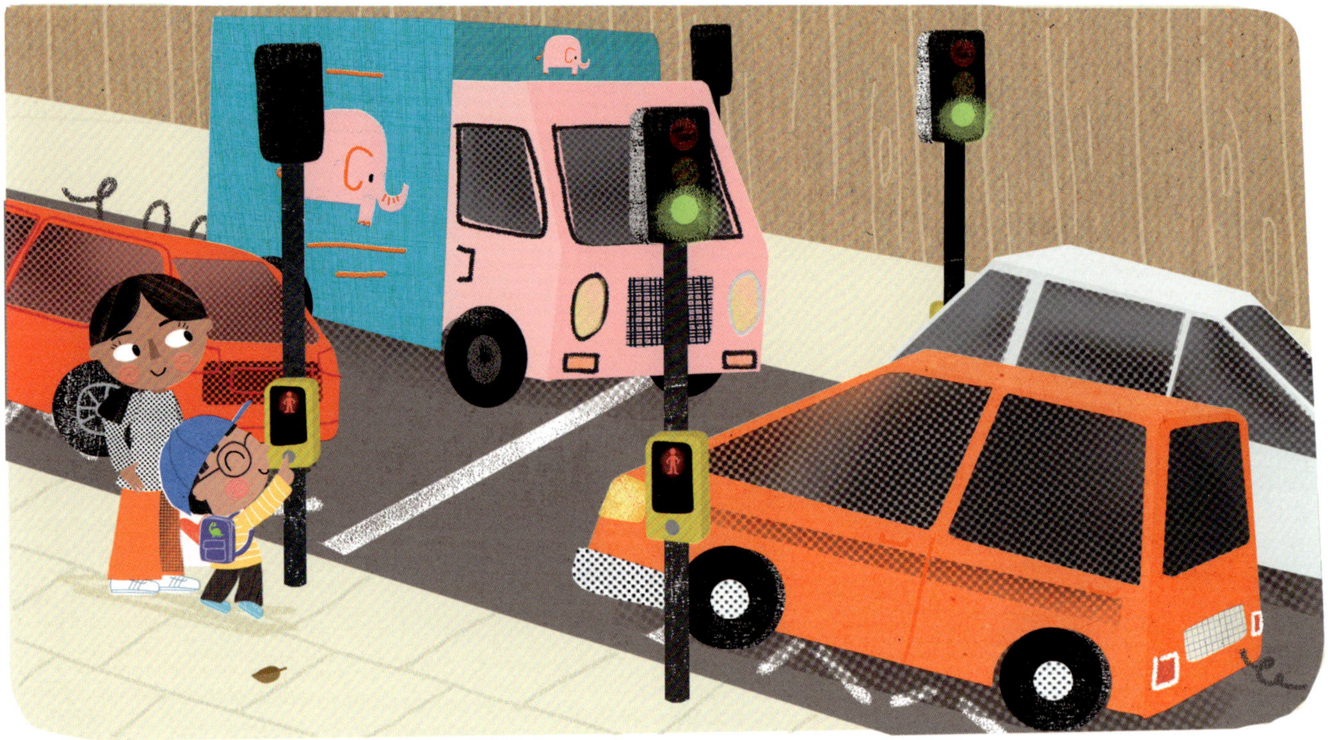

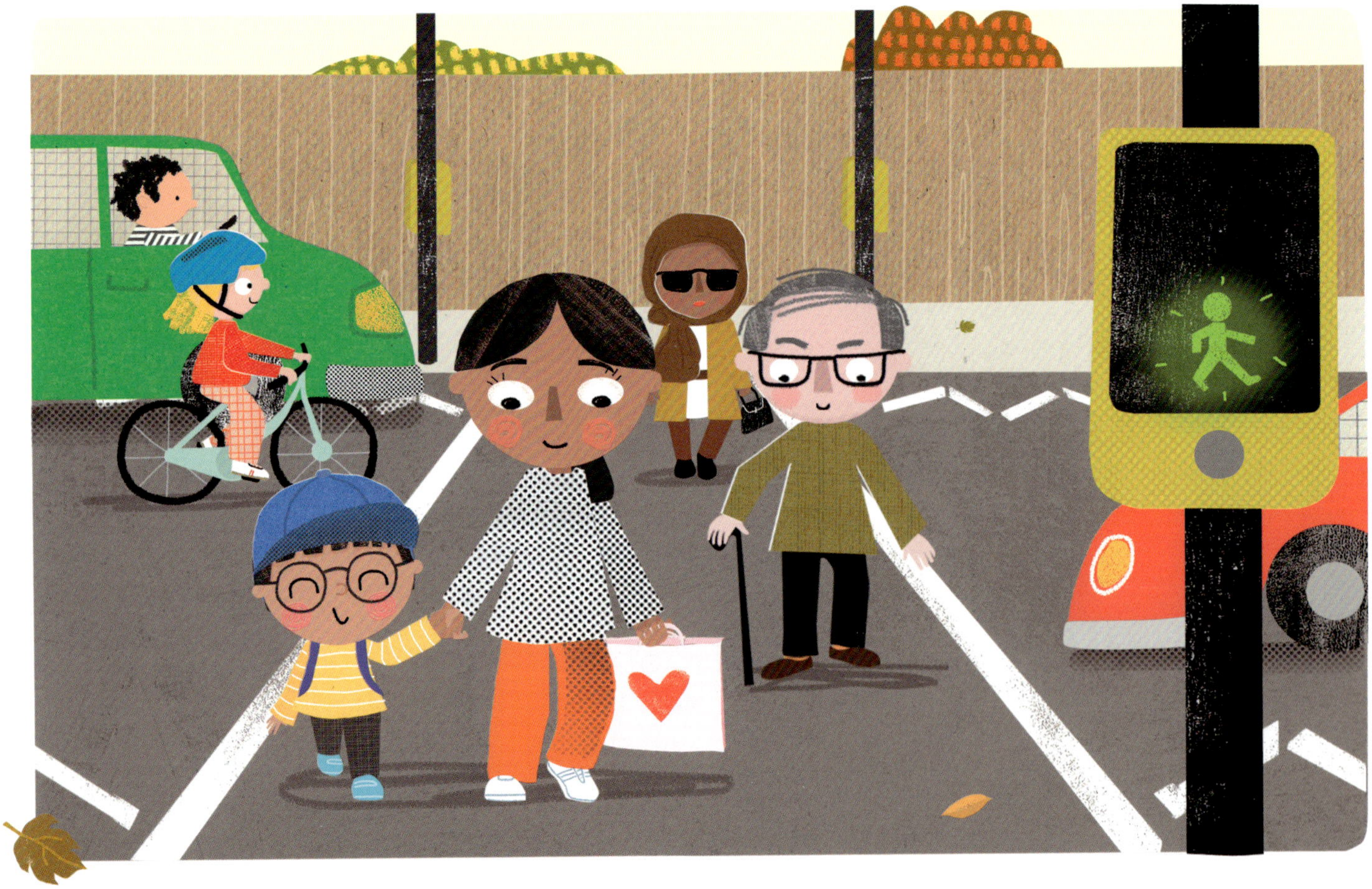

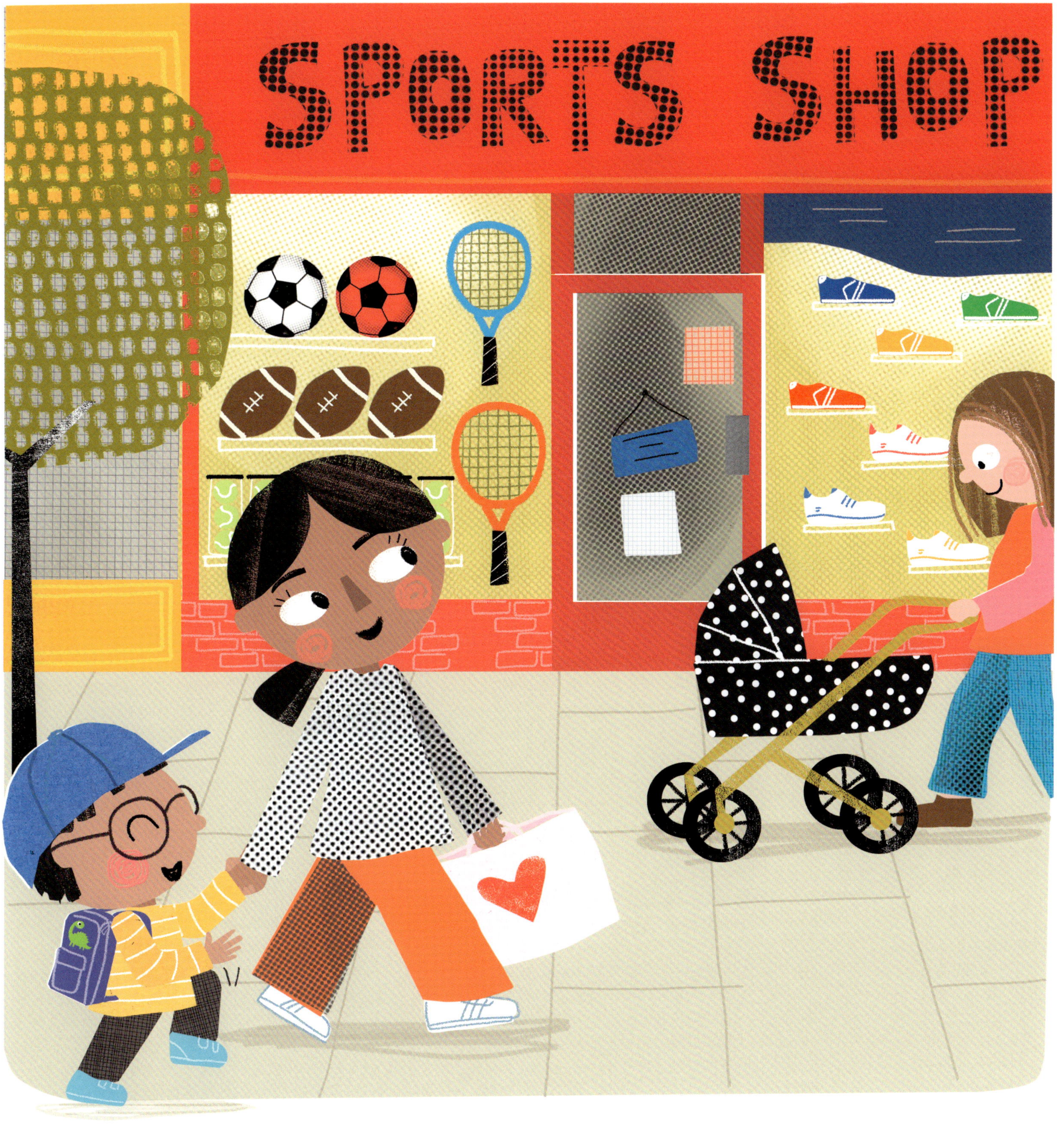
SPORTS SHOP

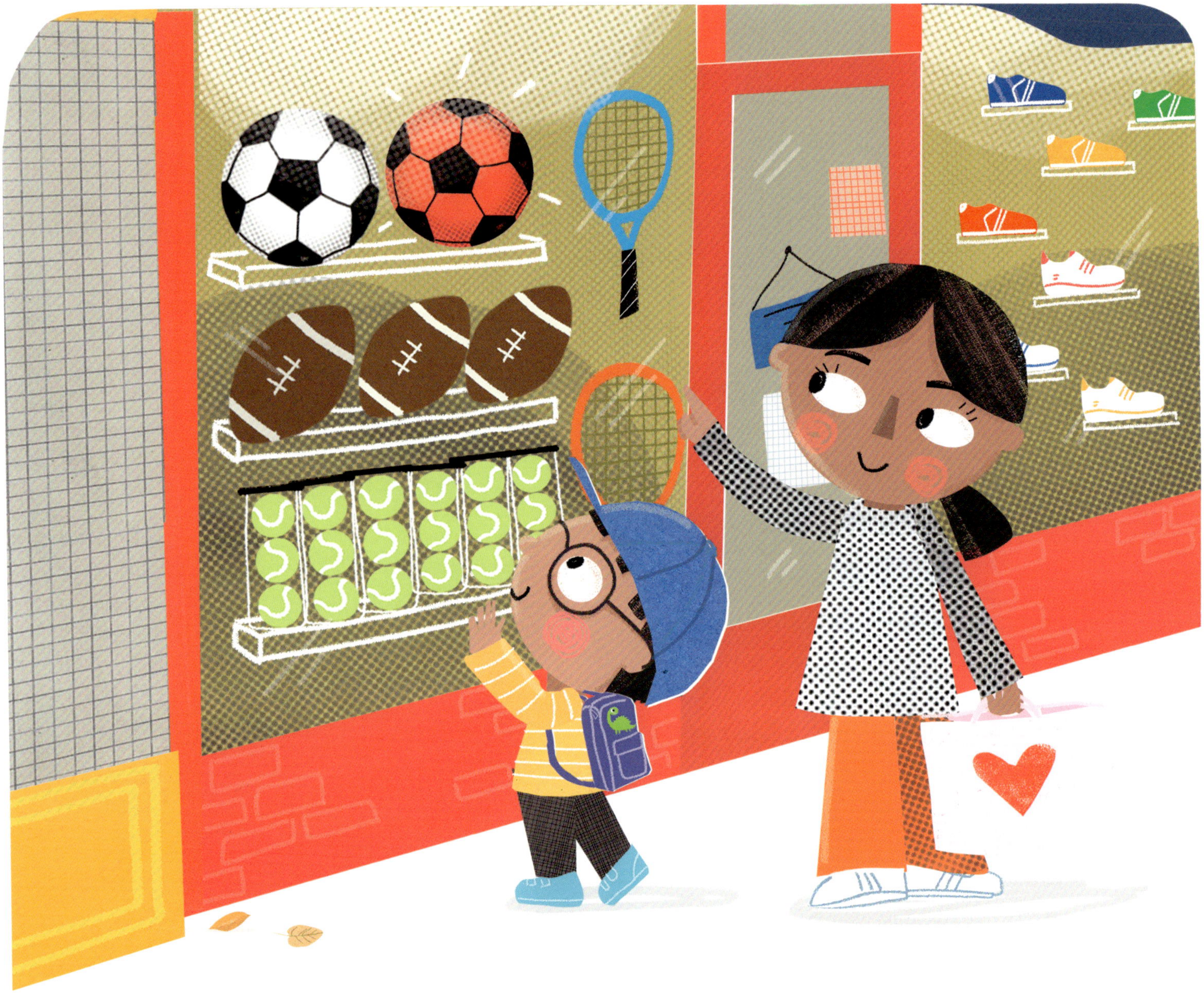

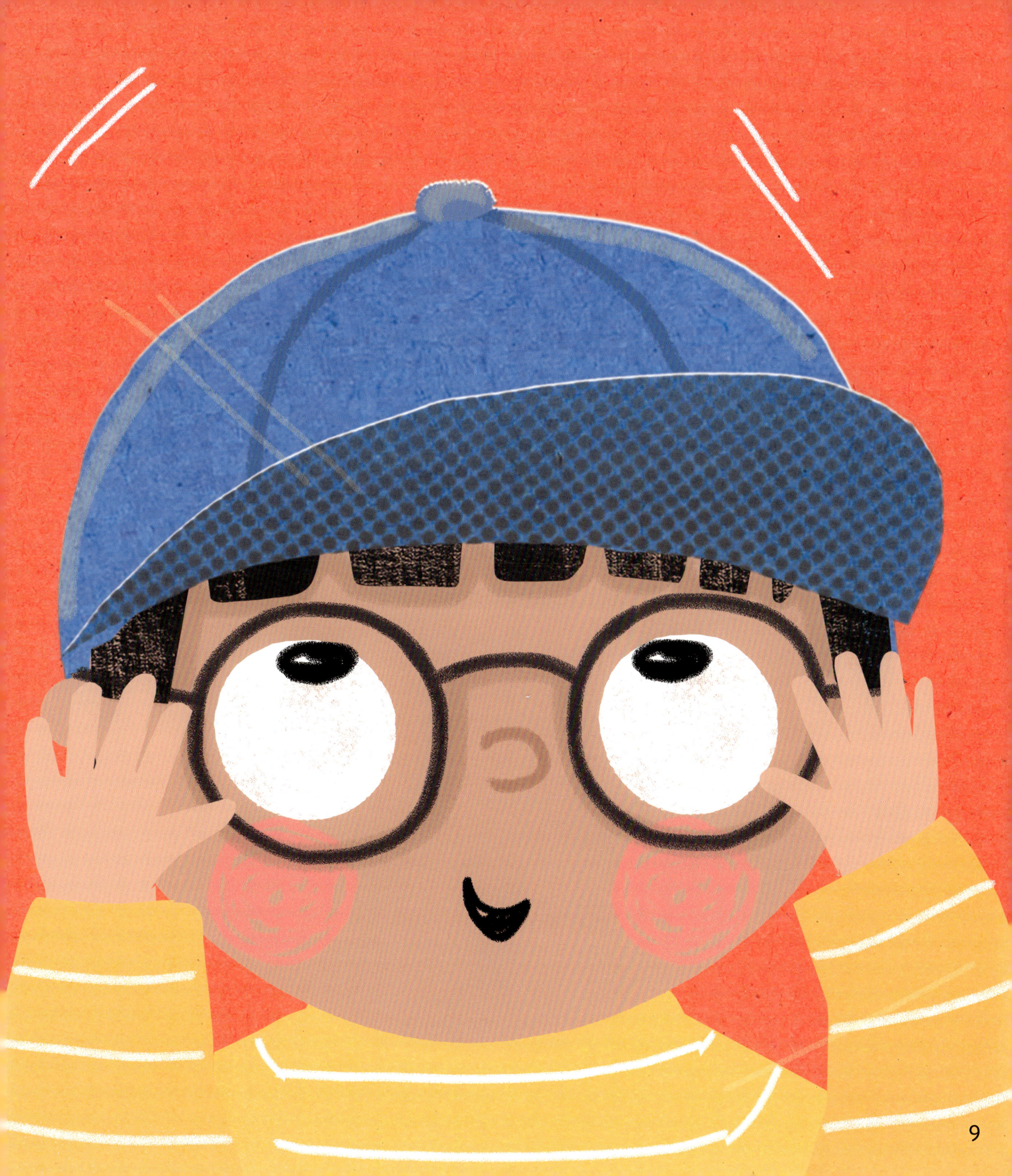

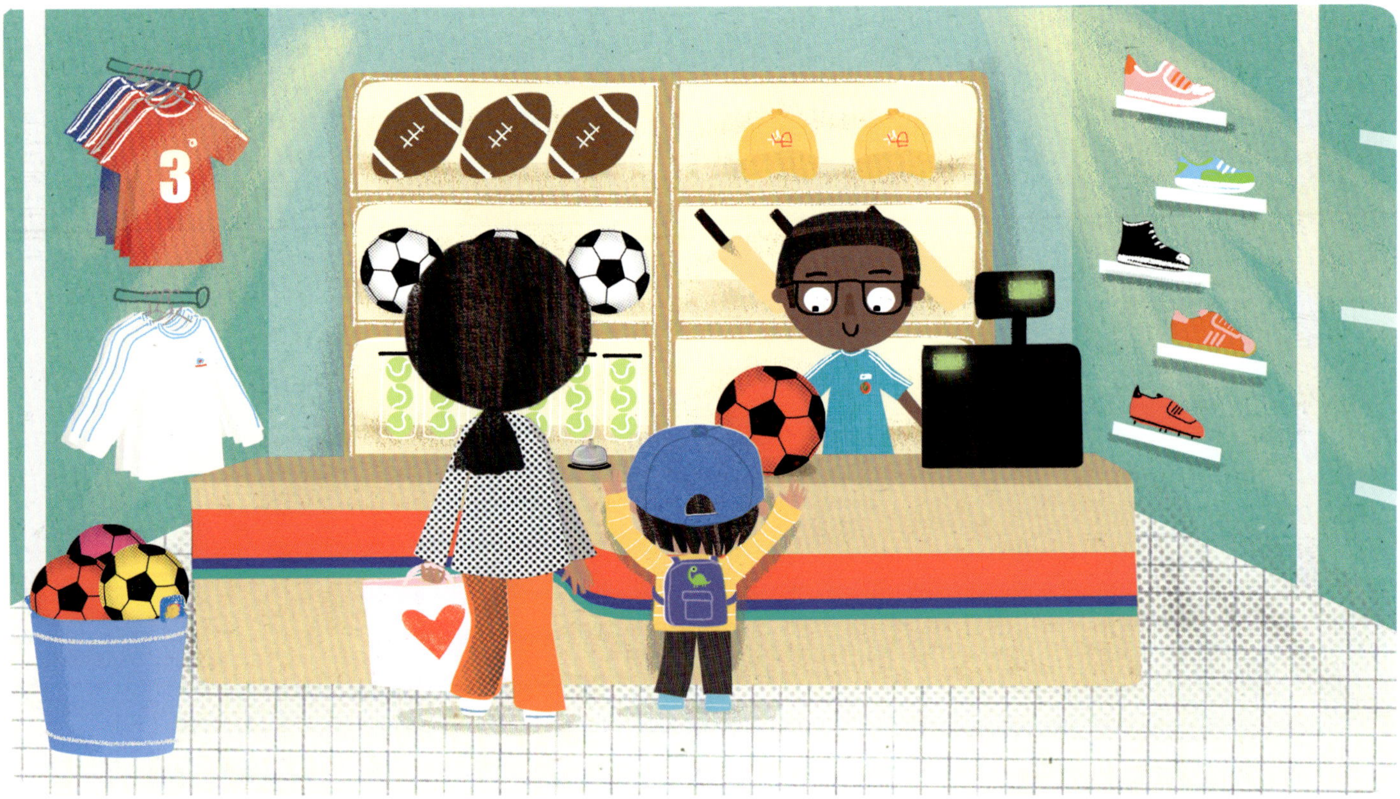

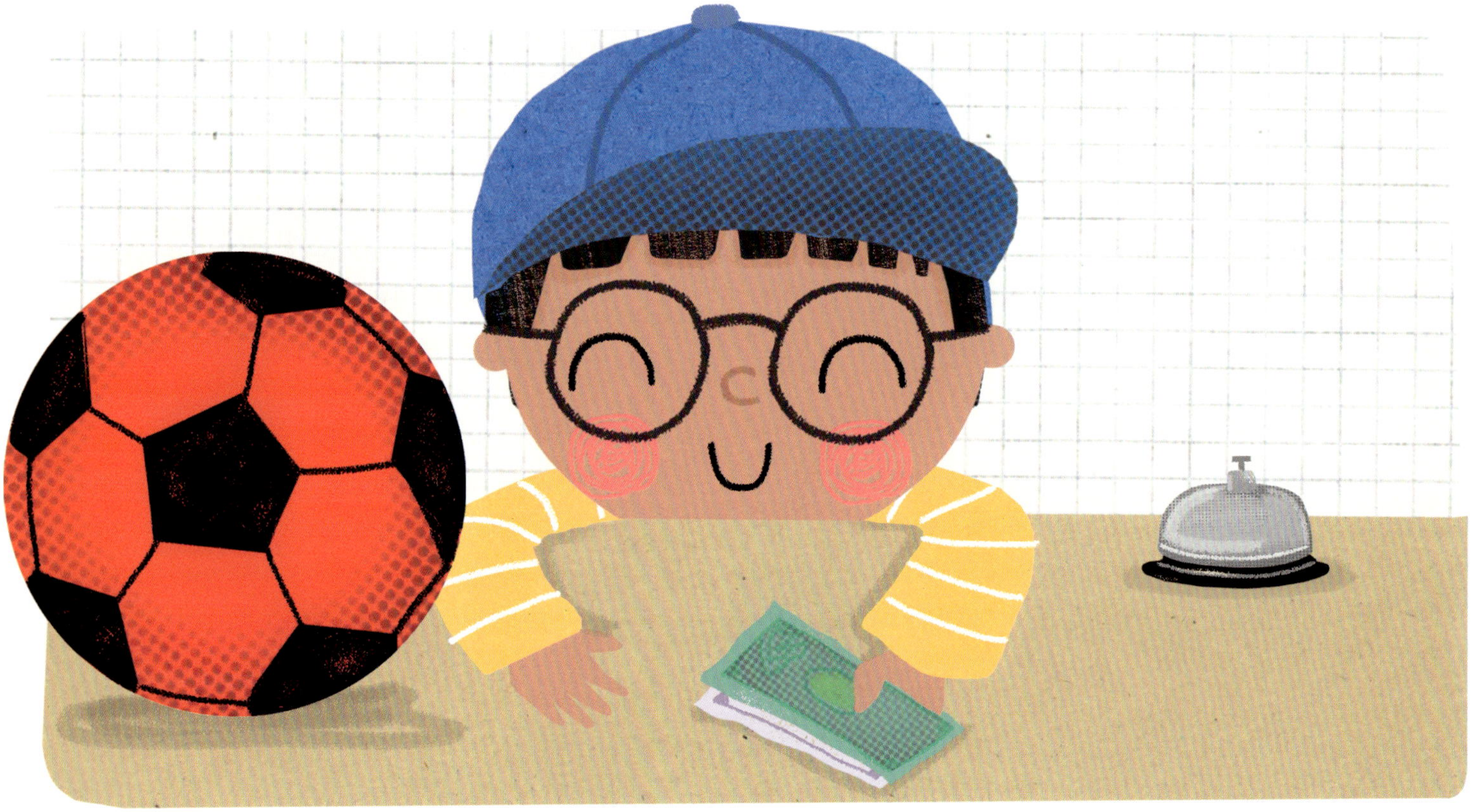

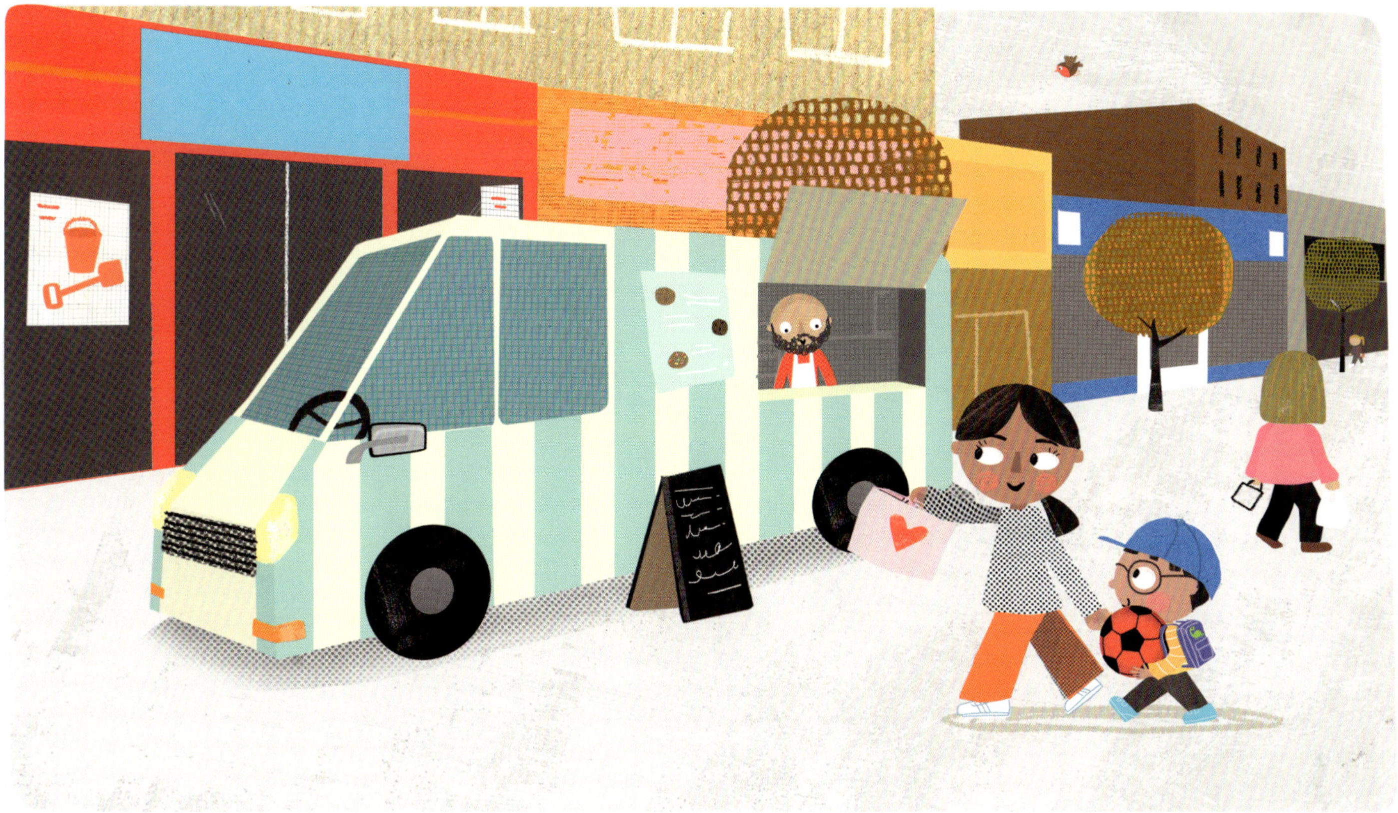

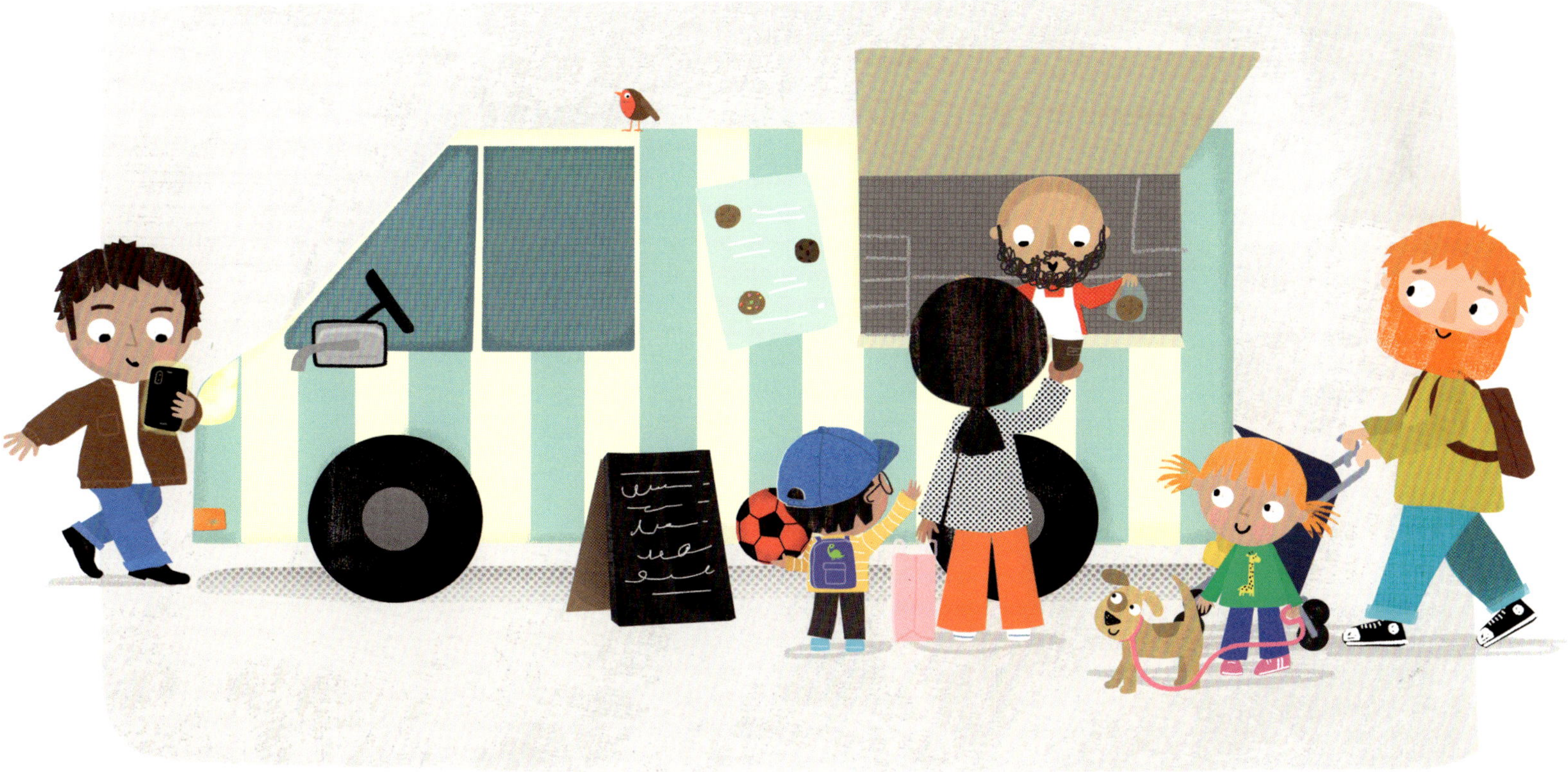

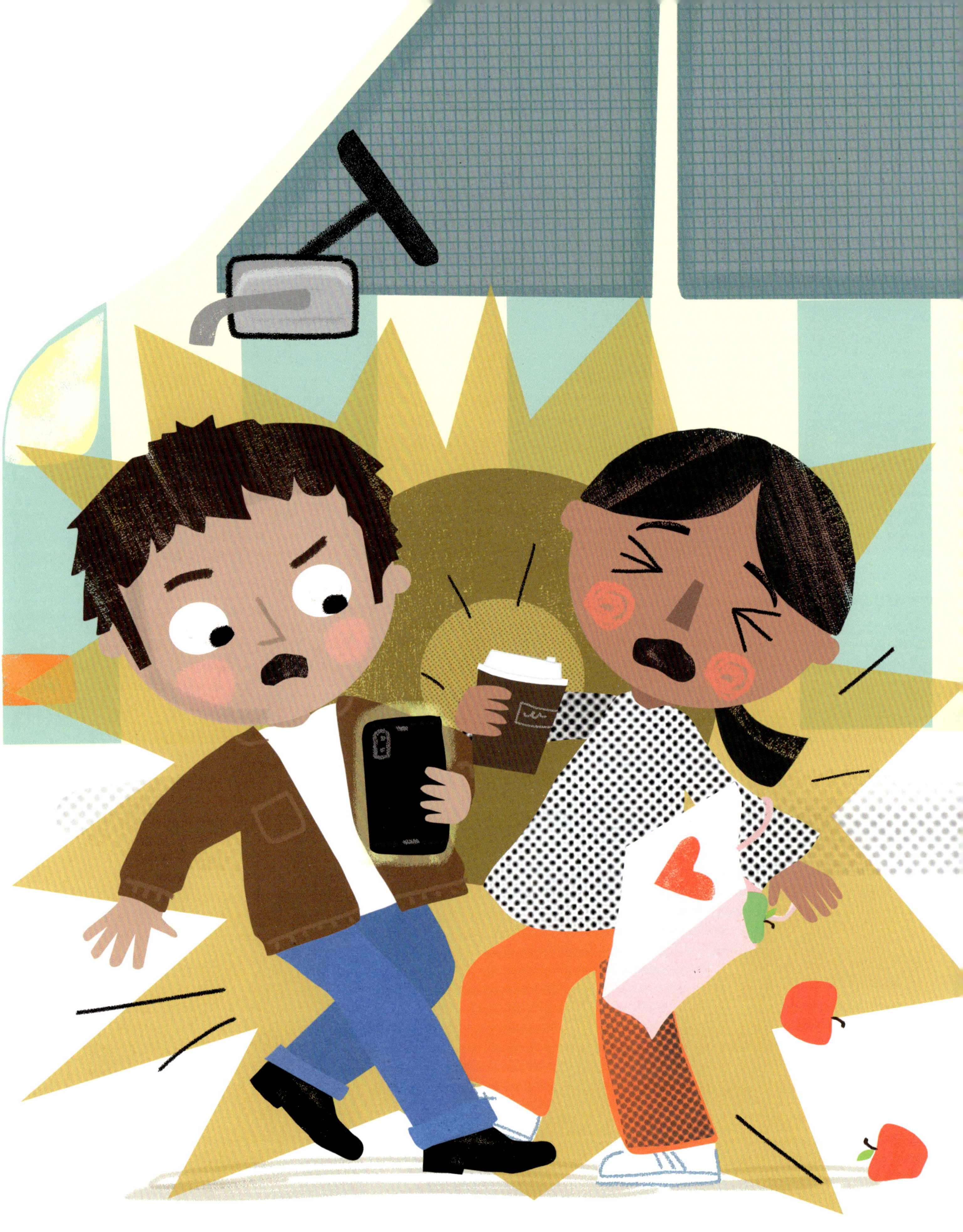

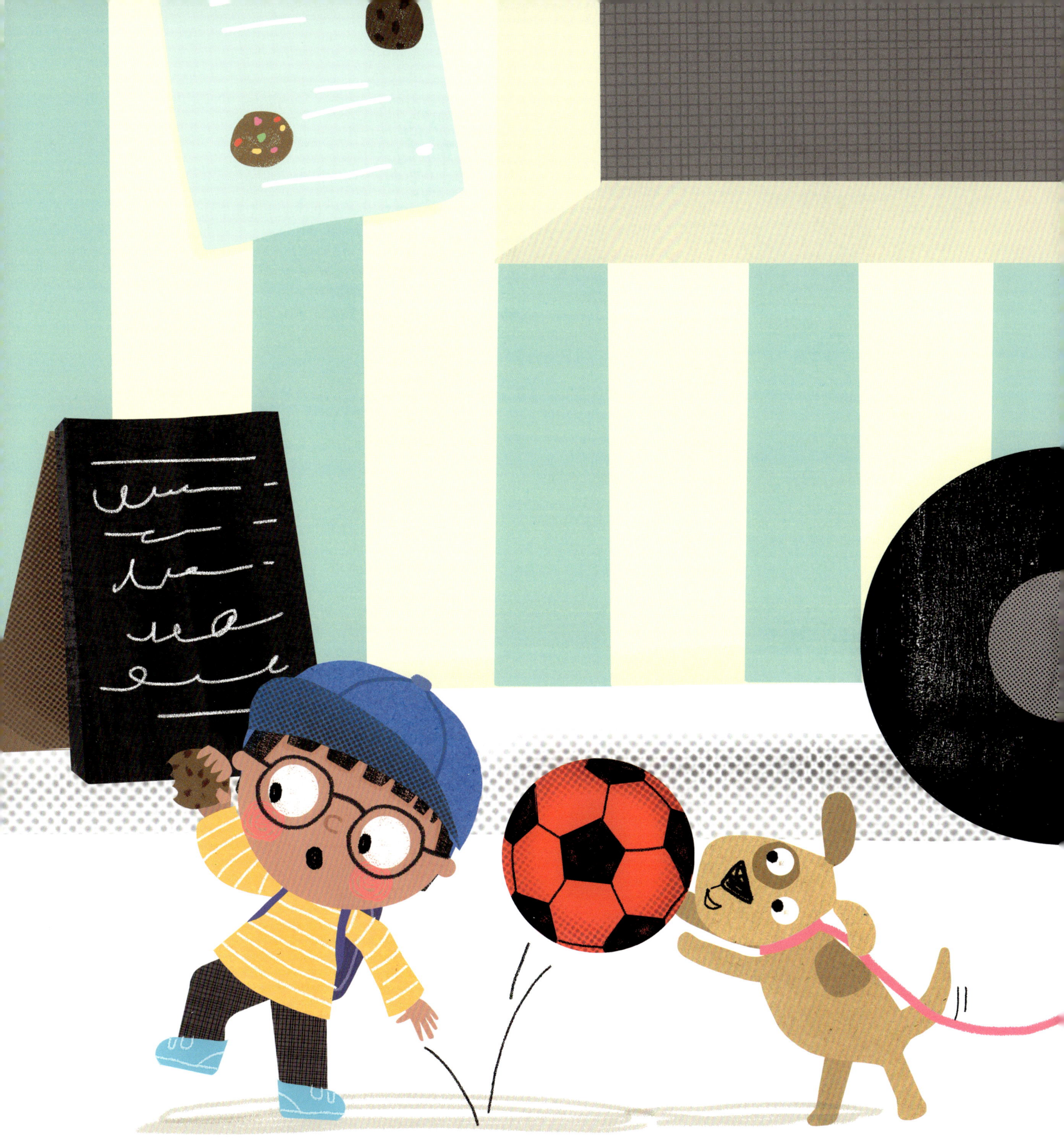

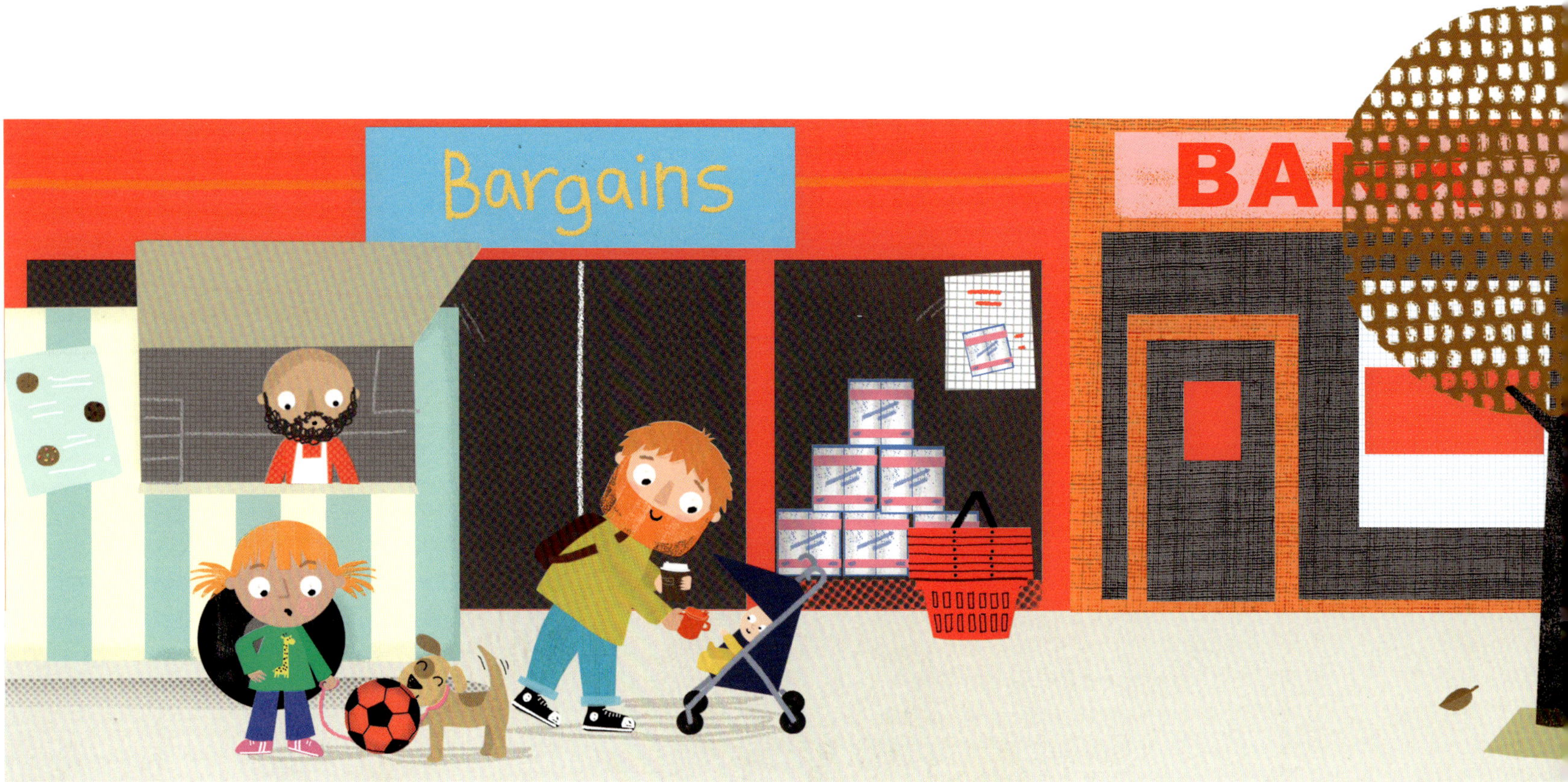
Bargains

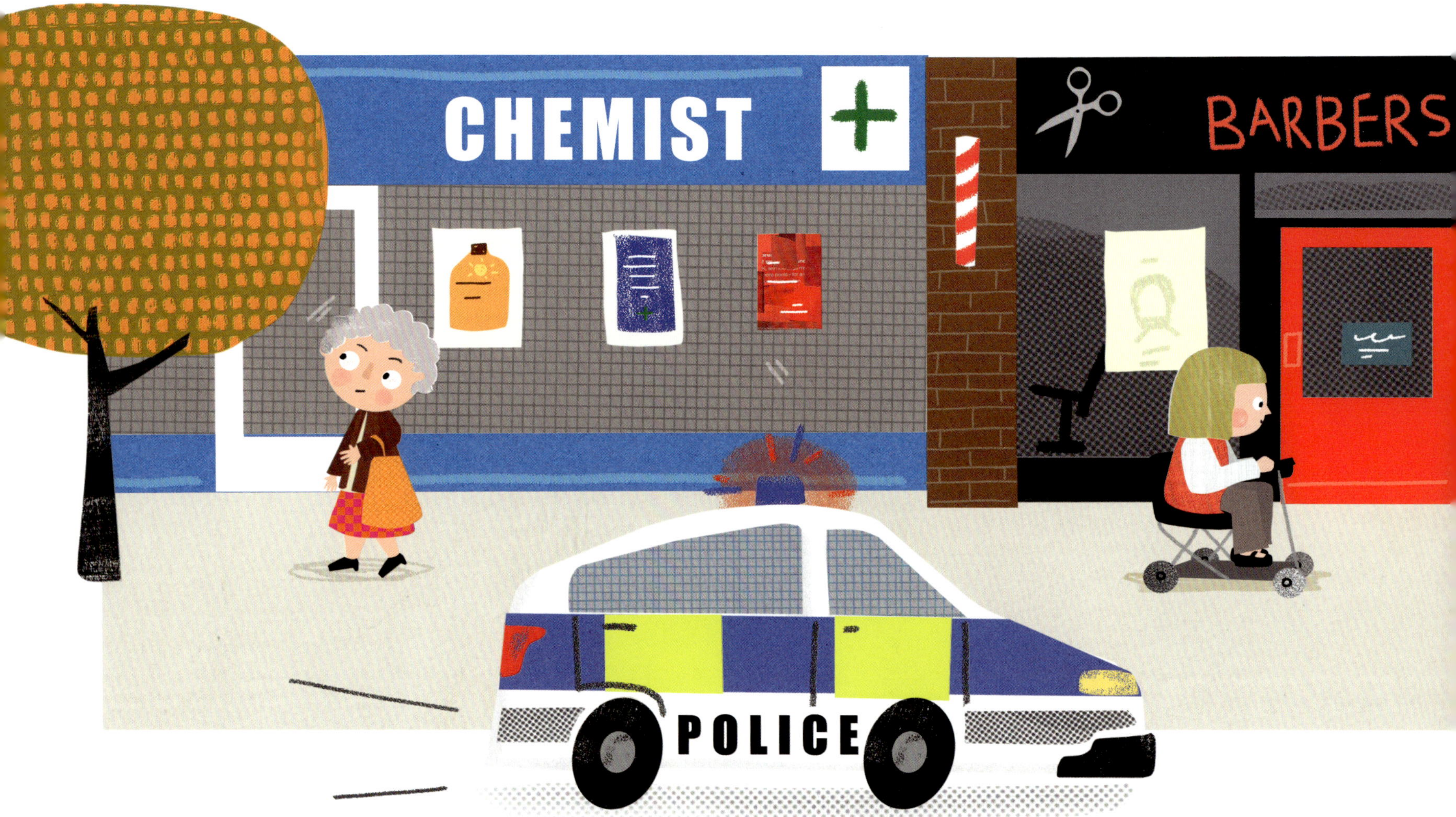
CHEMIST
BARBERS
POLICE

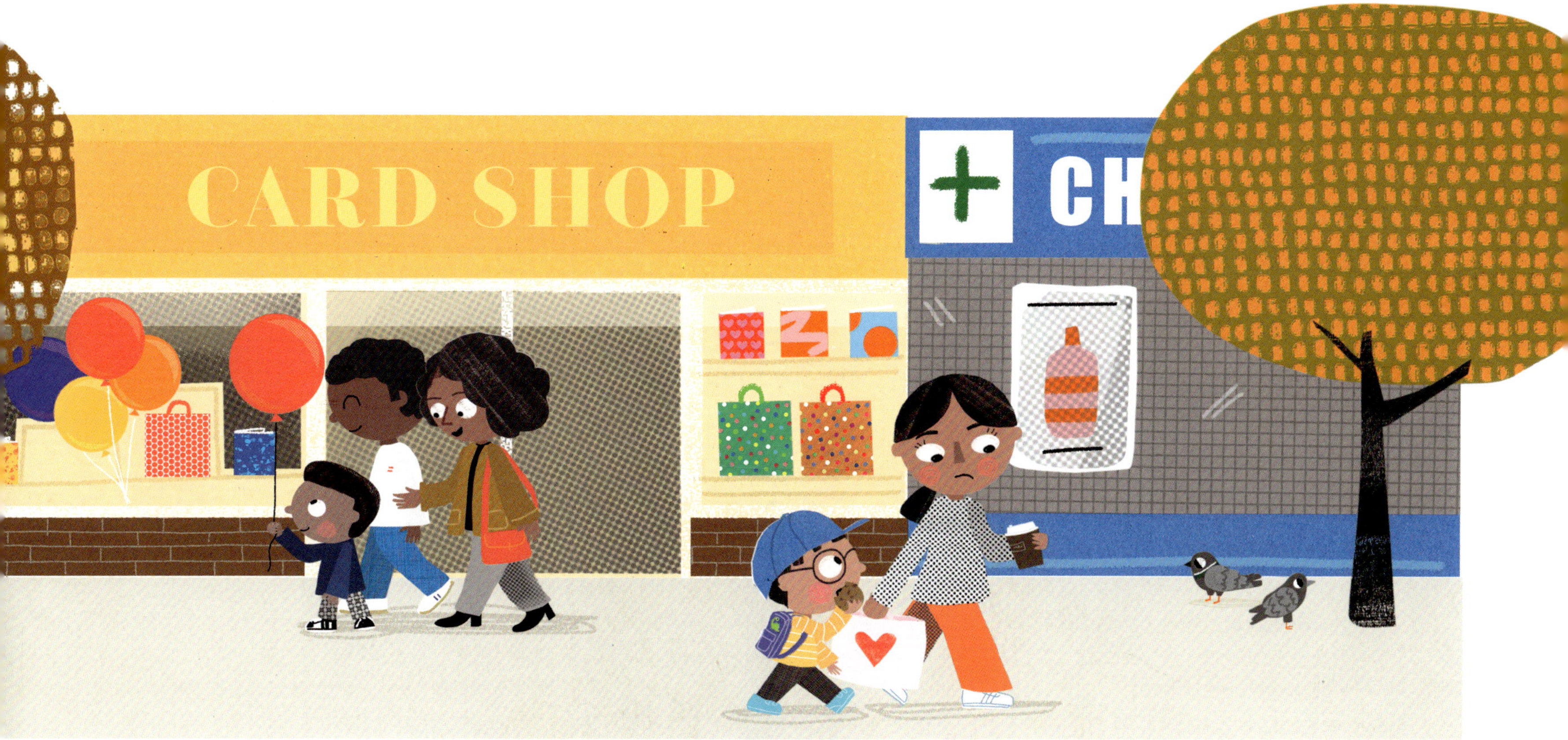
CARD SHOP

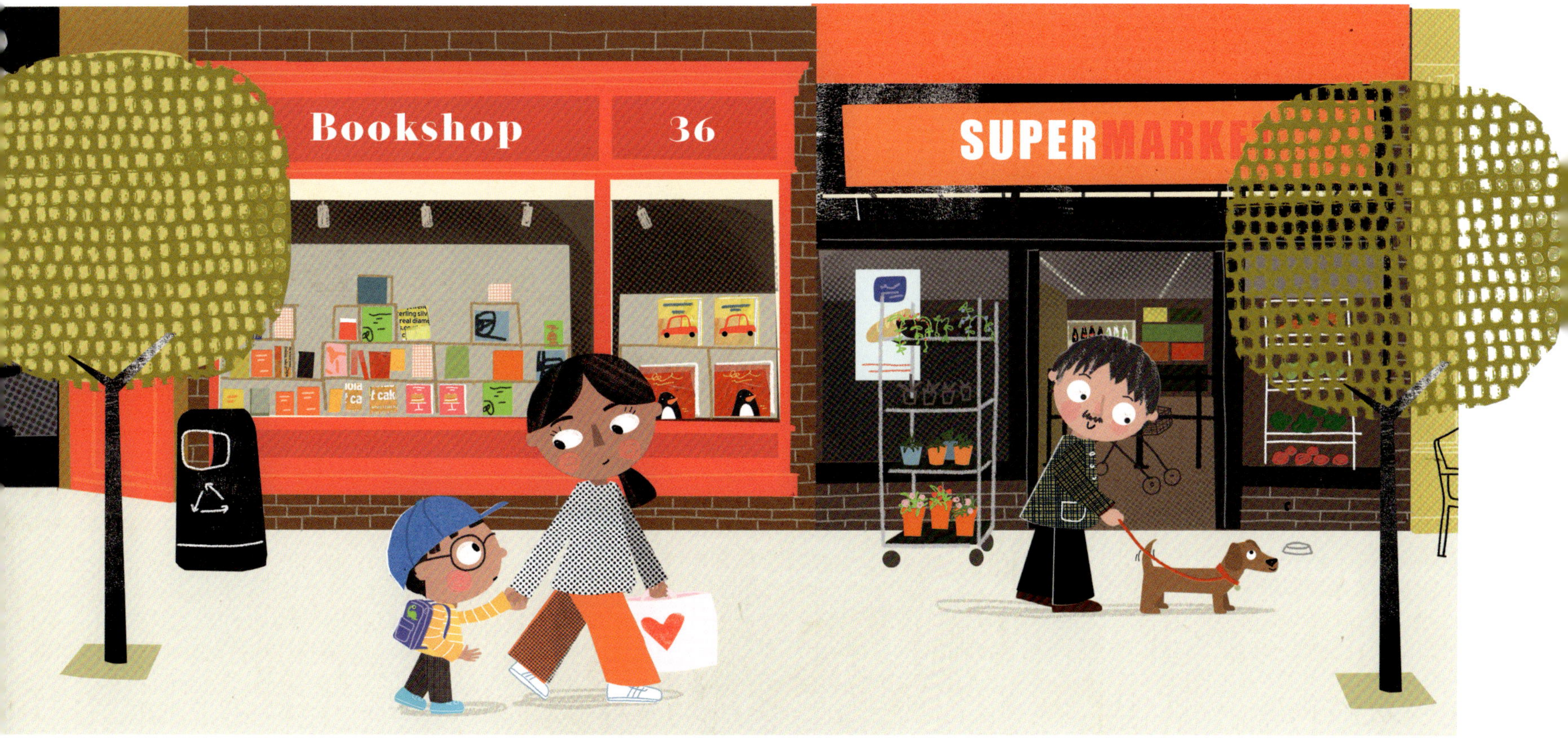
Bookshop
36
SUPER

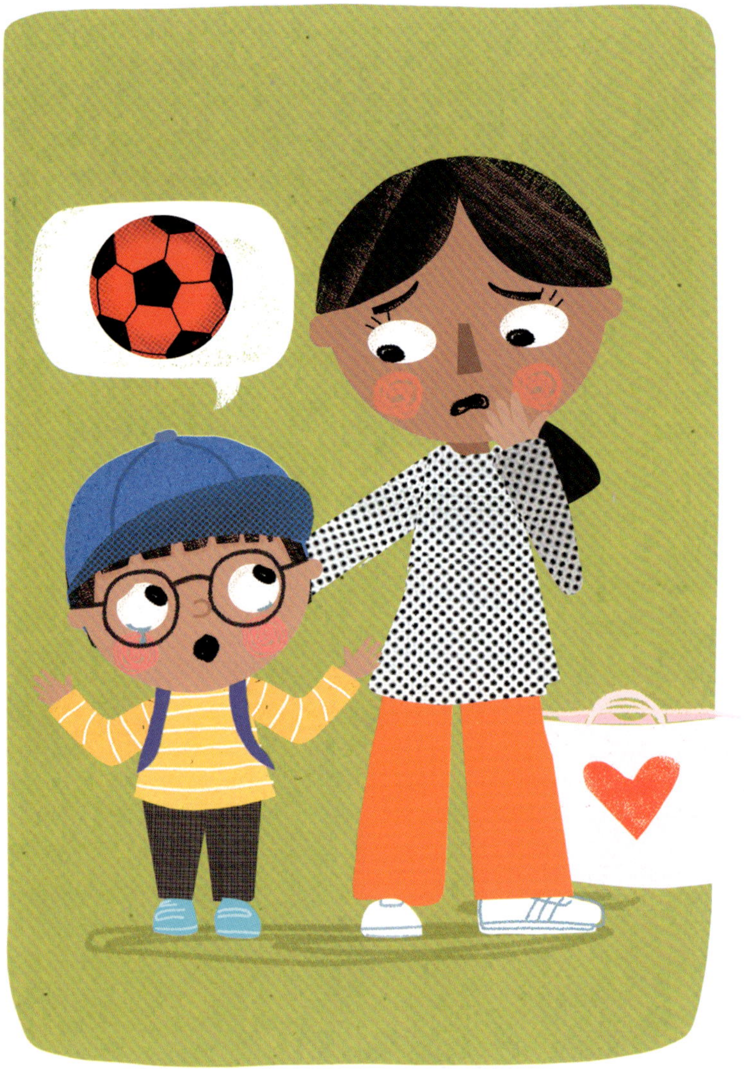

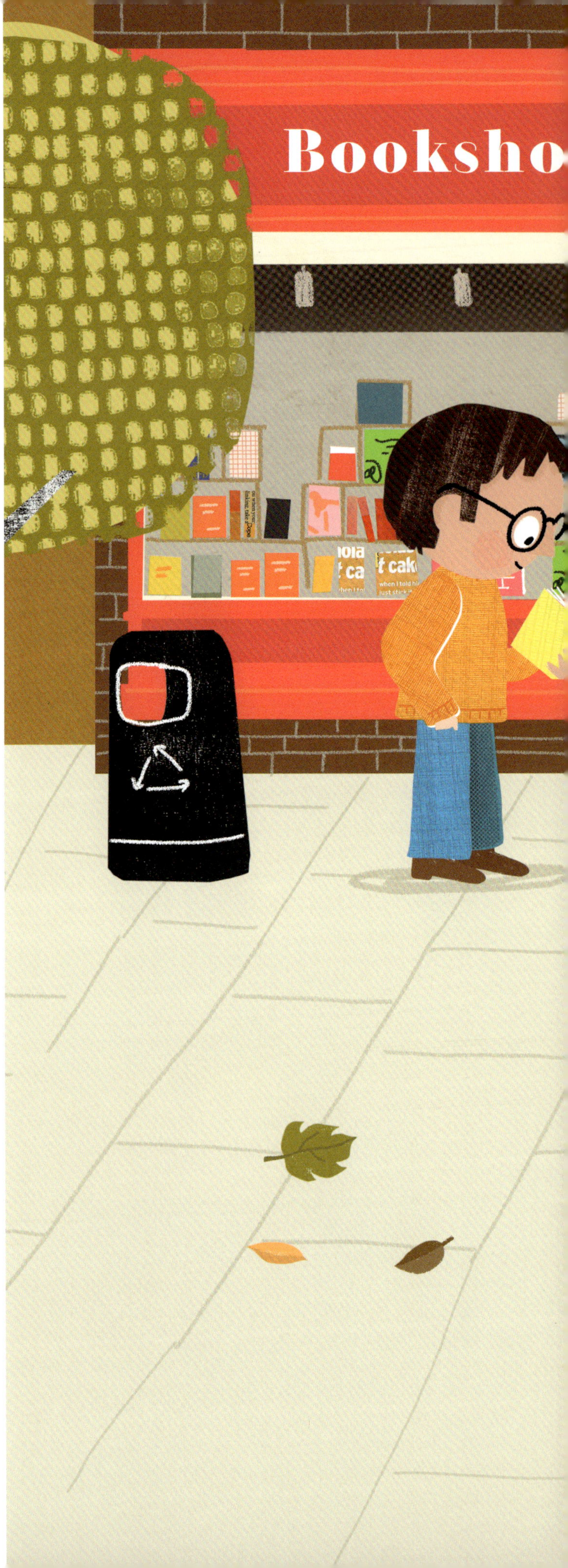
Booksho

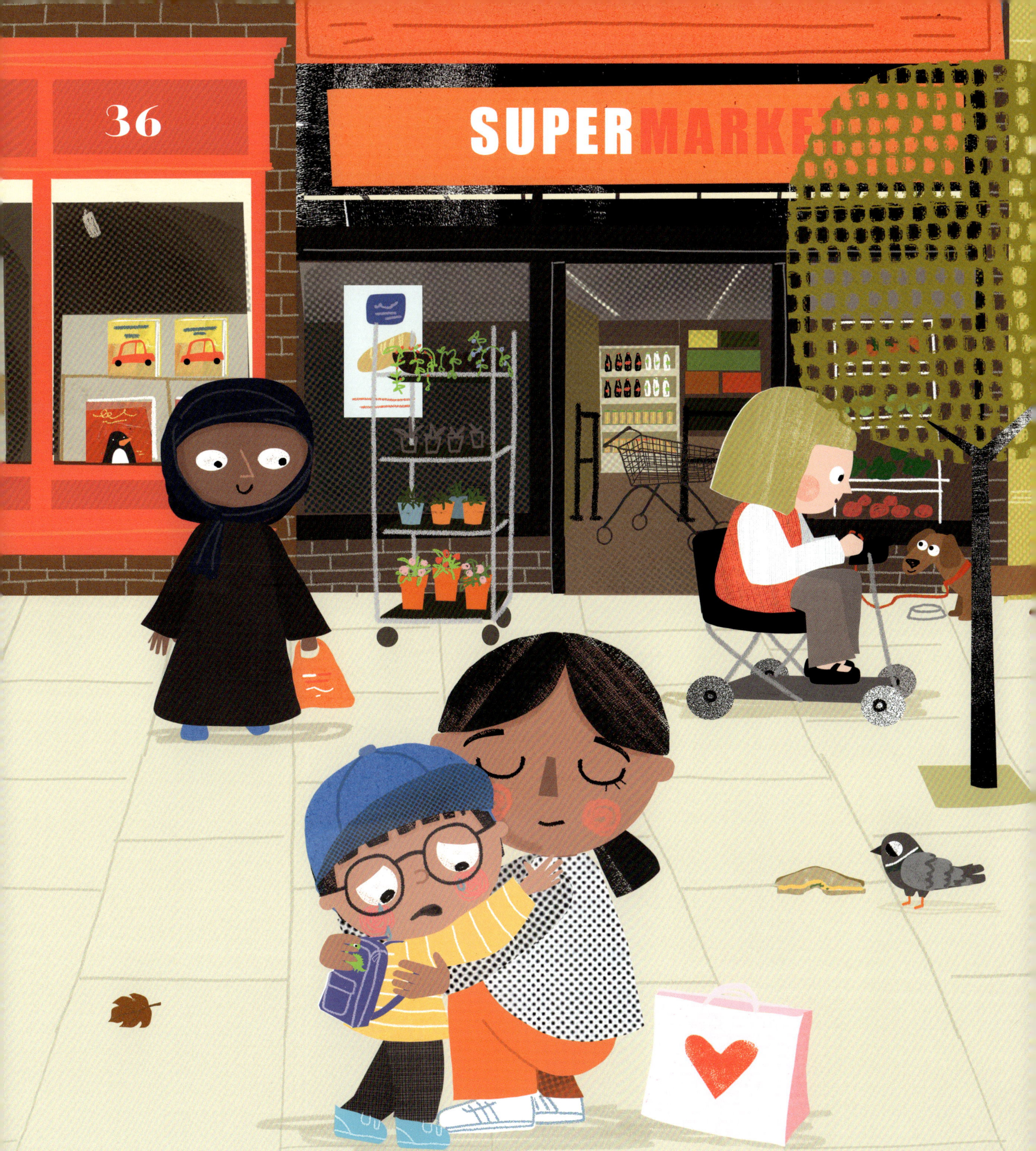
36
SUPERMARKE

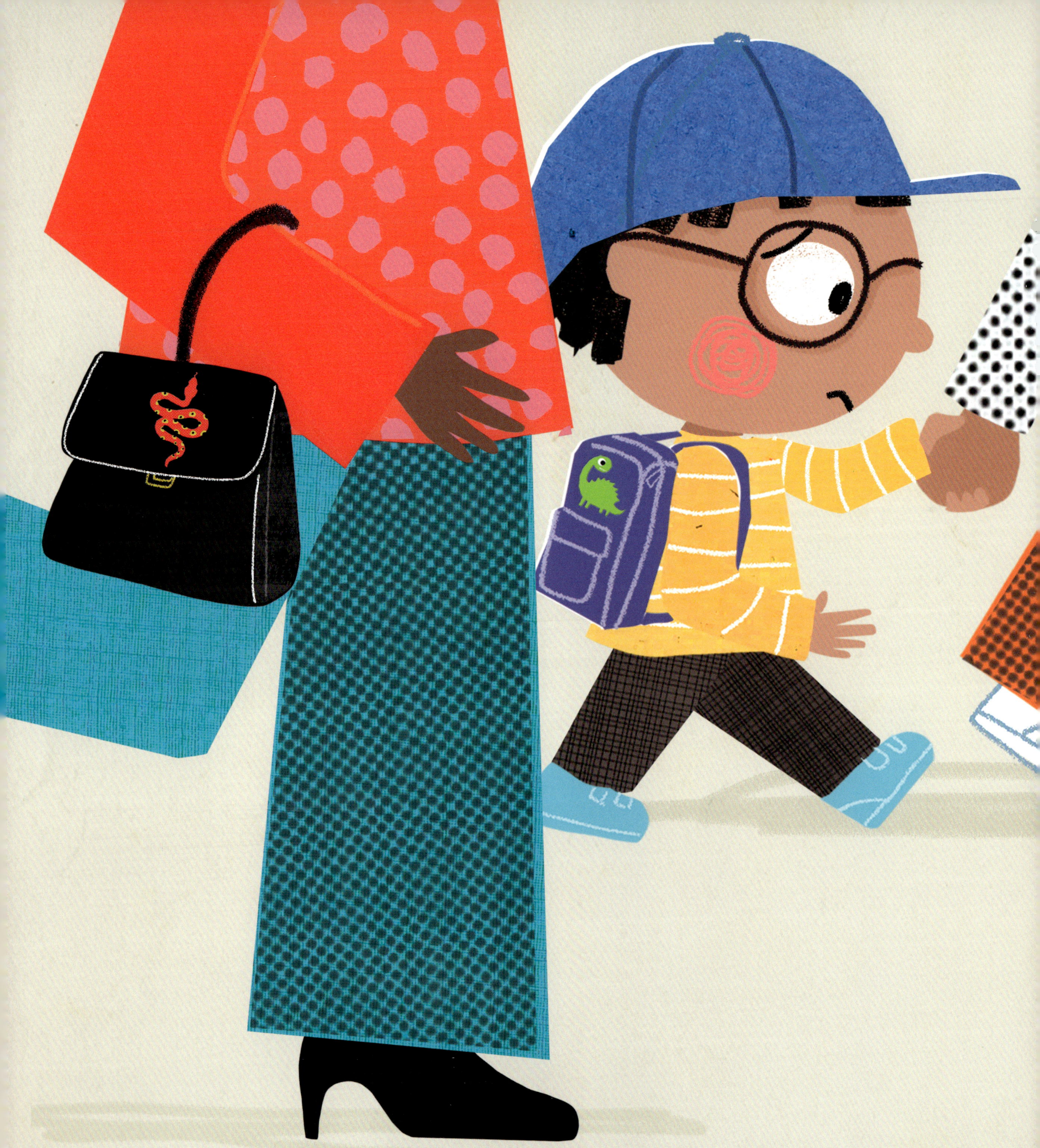

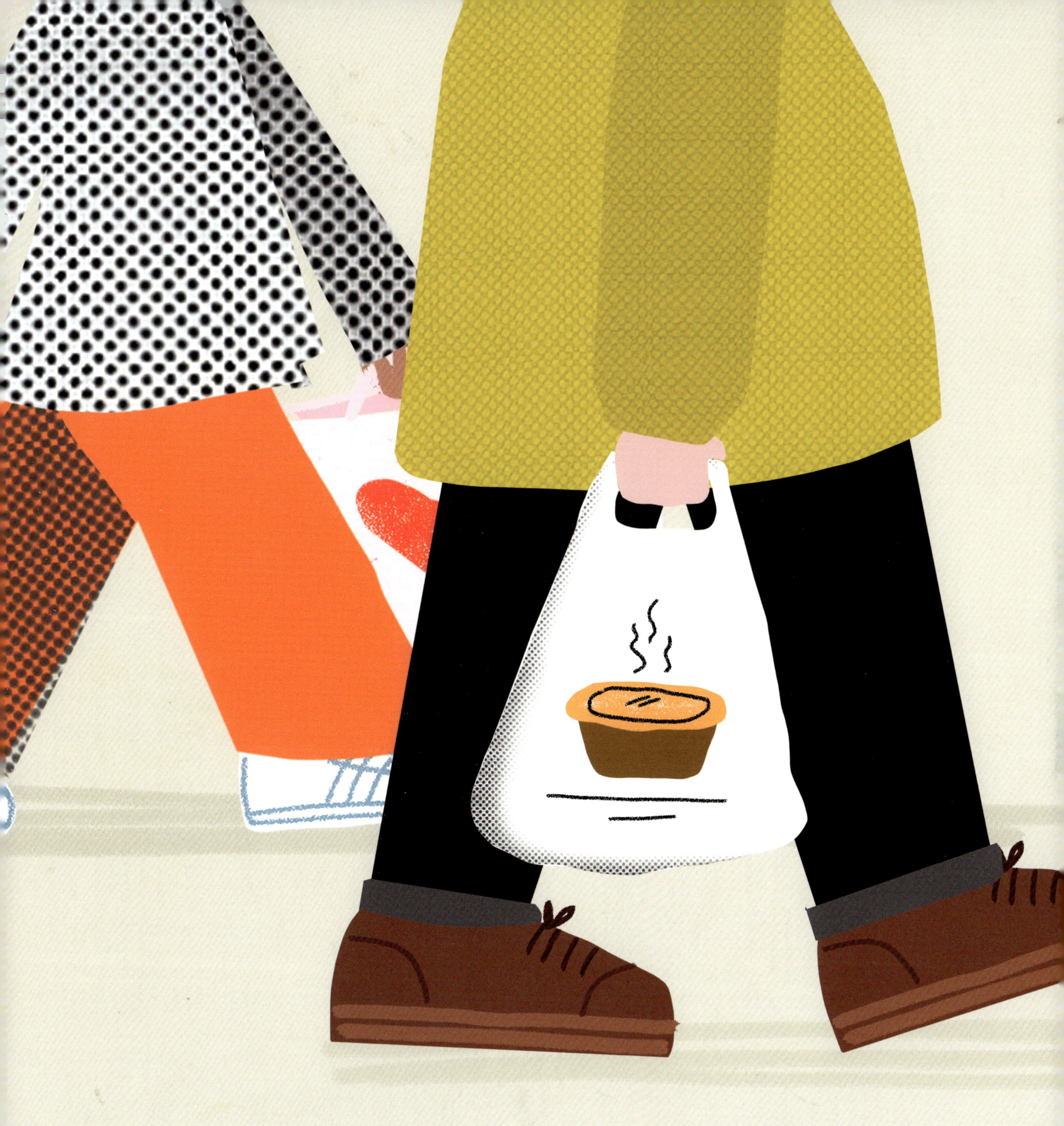

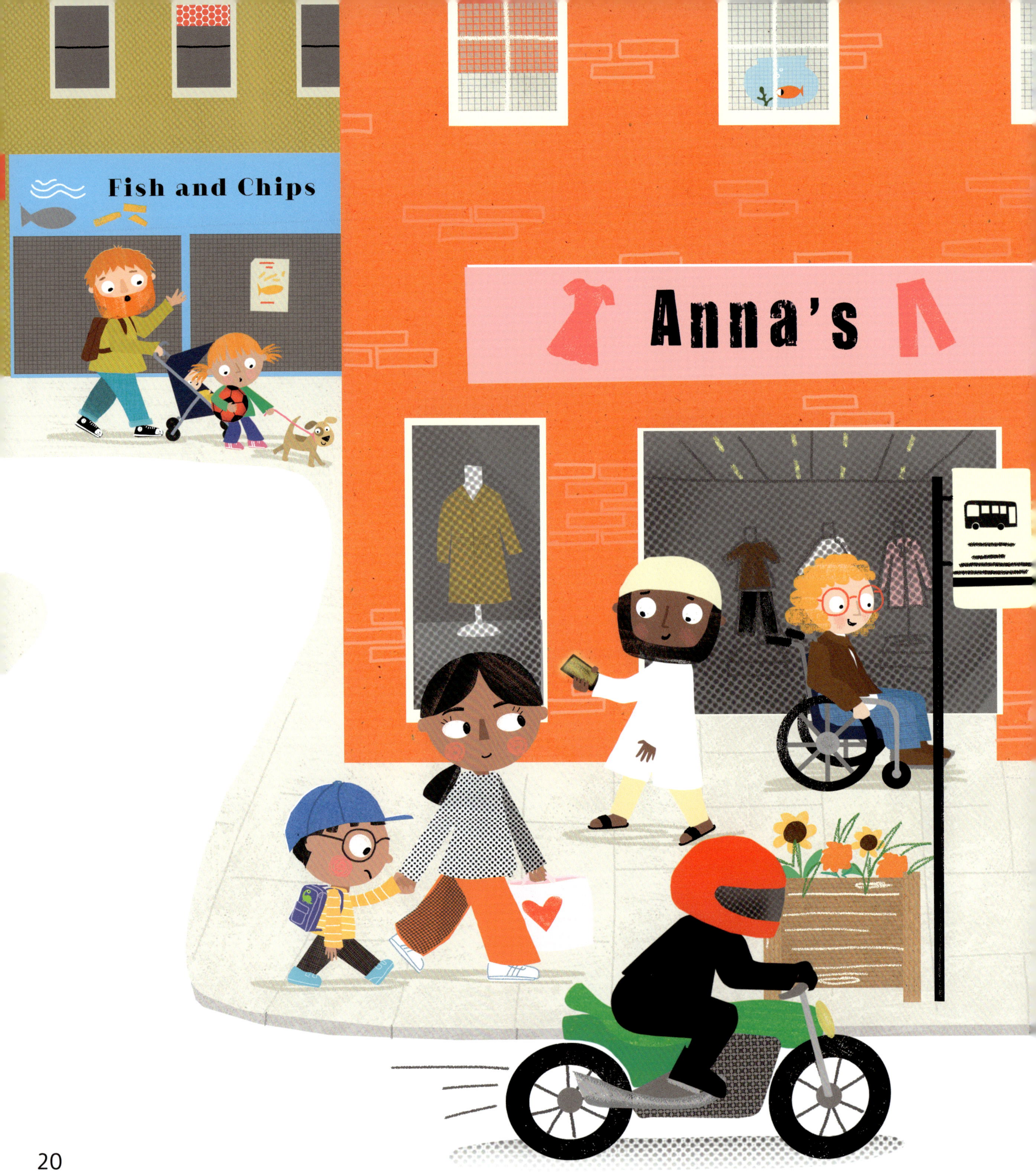
Fish and Chips
Anna's

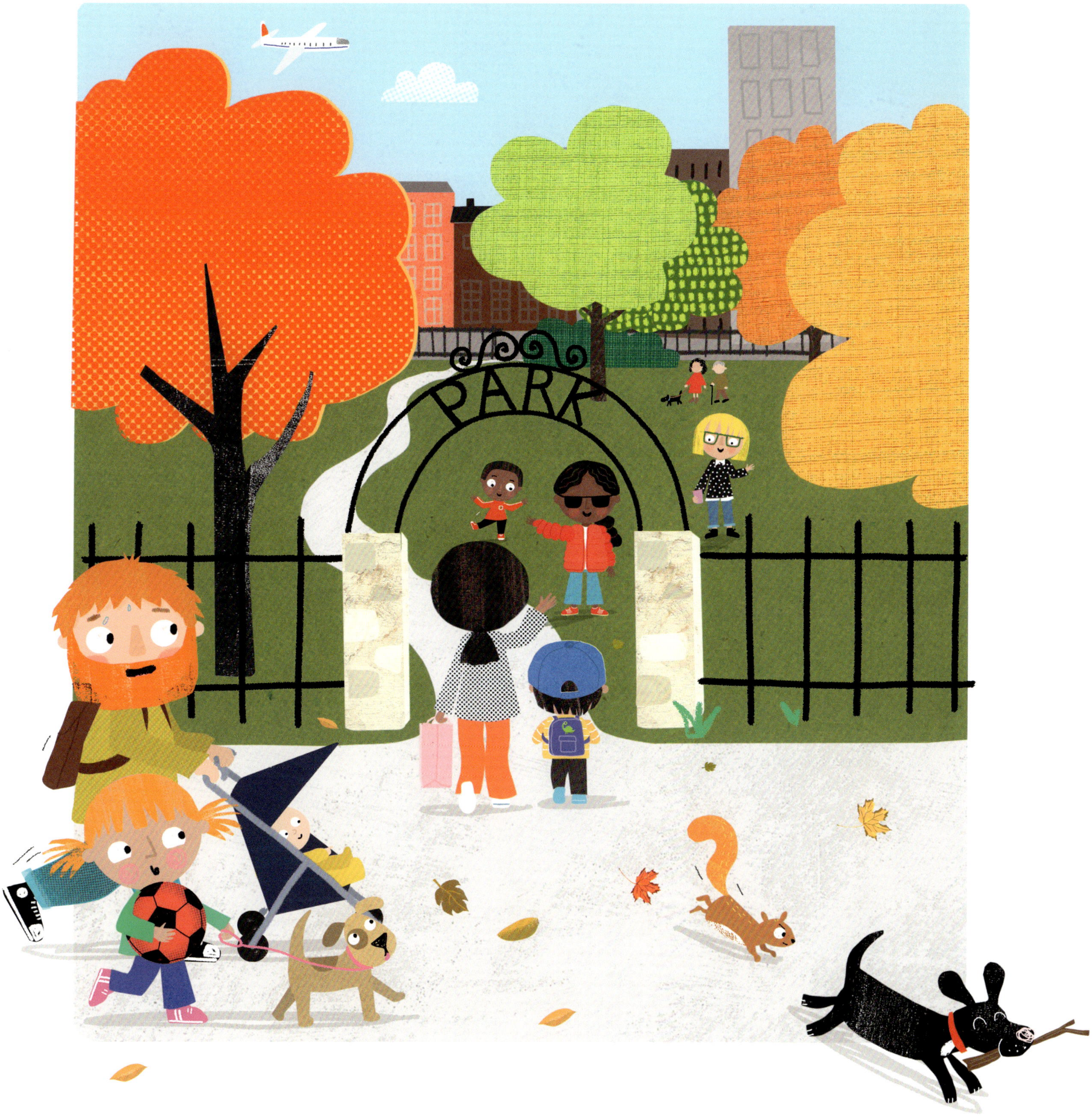
PARK

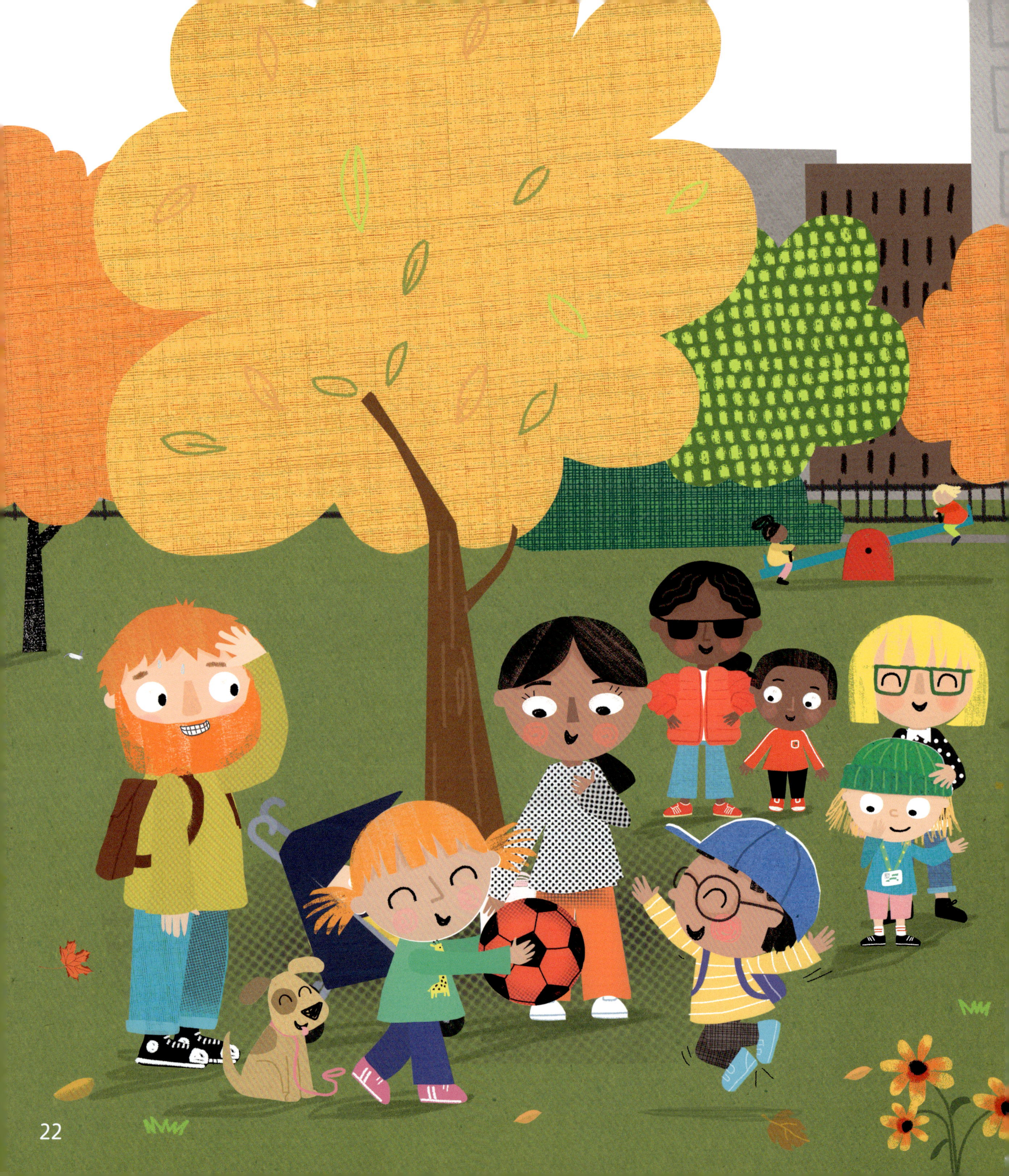

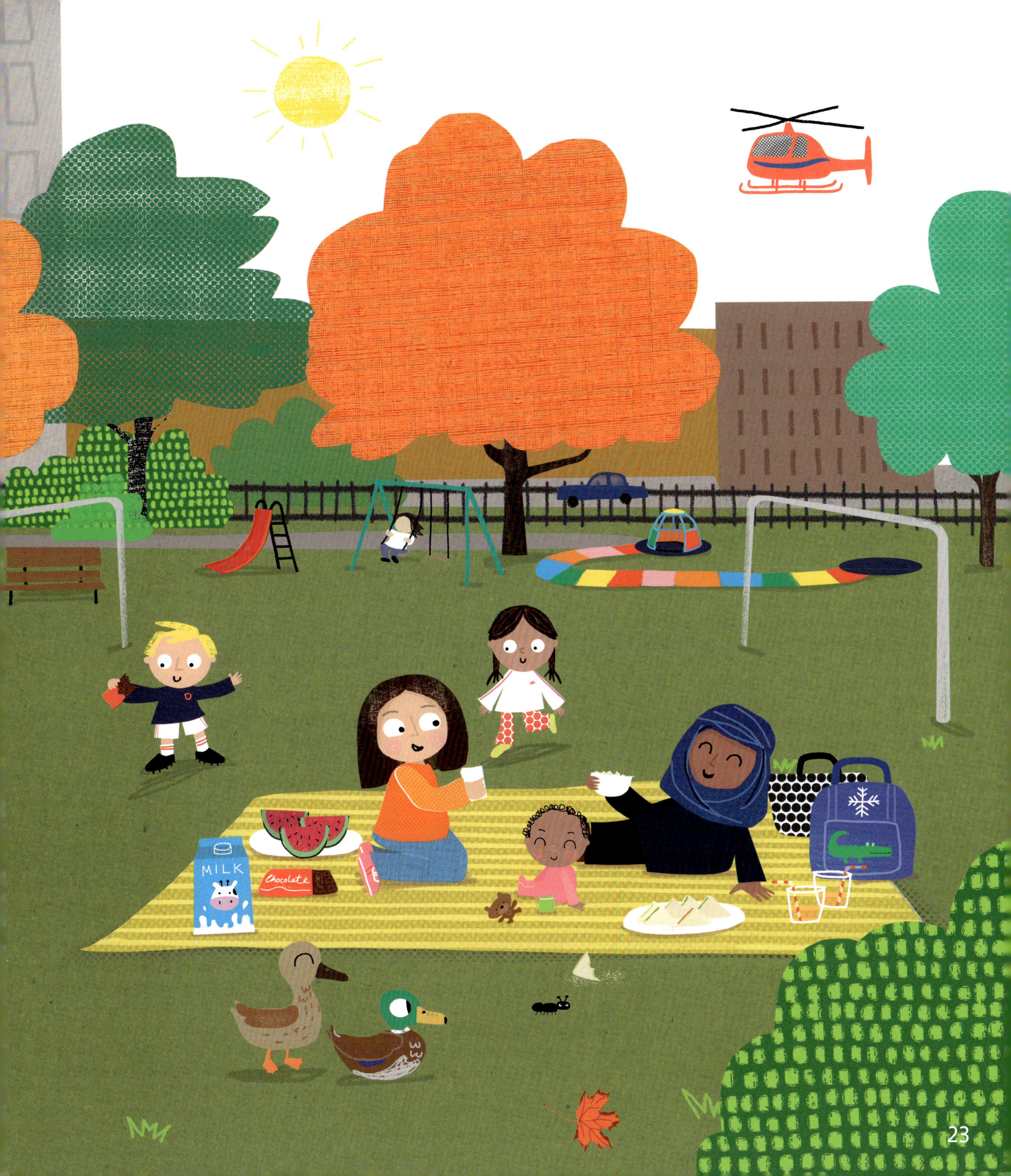
MILK
Chocolate

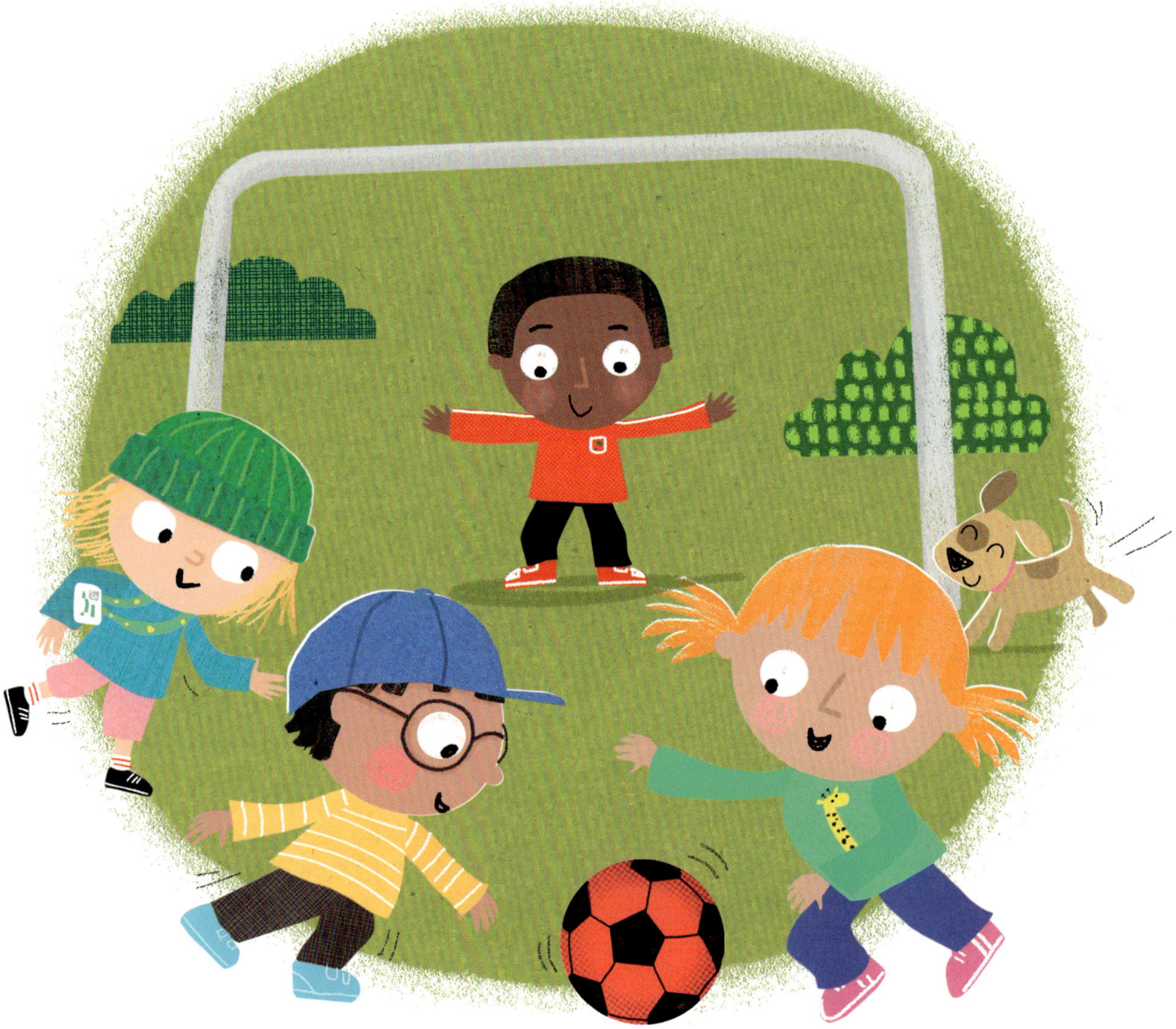